THE PAST

By Galway Kinnell

Poetry

What a Kingdom It Was   1960
Flower Herding on Mount Monadnock   1964
Body Rags   1968
First Poems 1946–1954   1971
The Book of Nightmares   1971
The Avenue Bearing the Initial of Christ
    into the New World: Poems 1946–64   1974
Mortal Acts, Mortal Words   1980
Selected Poems   1982
The Past   1985

Prose

Black Light   1966
Walking Down the Stairs: Selections from Interviews   1978
How the Alligator Missed Breakfast (for children)   1982

Translations

Bitter Victory (novel by René Hardy)   1956
The Poems of François Villon   1965
On the Motion and Immobility of Douve
    (poems by Yves Bonnefoy)   1968
Lackawanna Elegy (poems by Yvan Goll)   1970
The Poems of François Villon (second version)   1977

THE PAST

GALWAY KINNELL

HOUGHTON MIFFLIN COMPANY

Boston

Library of Congress Cataloging in Publication Data

Kinnell, Galway, date.
  The past.
  I. Title.
PS3521.I582P3 1985   811'.54   85–14211
ISBN 0–395–39385–X
ISBN 0–395–39386–8 (pbk.)

PRINTED IN THE UNITED STATES OF AMERICA

HAD 12 11 10 9 8 7 6 5 4 3

The poems in this book first appeared in journals and magazines as follows:
American Poetry Review — The Fundamental Project of Technology, On the
Oregon Coast, The Waking; *Antaeus* — Conception, December Day in
Honolulu, Driftwood from a Ship, The Man Splitting Wood in the Day-
break; *Apparitions* — Cemetery Angels, Farm Picture; *The Atlantic* — The
Past; *Kenyon Review* — Fire in Luna Park, Last Holy Fragrance; *Mother
Jones* — The Road Between Here and There; *The Nation* — Break of Day,
Prayer; *New Letters* — The Olive Wood Fire; *The New Yorker* — First
Day of the Future, Middle of the Night, The Seekonk Woods, The Shroud;
Paris Review — Chamberlain's Porch, The Frog Pond, The Geese, The Old
Life; *Scripsi* — The Ferry Stopping at MacMahon's Point; *Southwest Re-
view* — Milk; *Verse* — The Angel, The Sow Piglet's Escapes.

FOR INÉS

CONTENTS

PART I

PART II

PART III

PART I

THE ROAD BETWEEN HERE AND THERE

Here I heard the terrible chaste snorting of hogs trying to re-enter the underearth.

Here I came into the curve too fast, on ice, and being new to these winters, touched the brake and sailed into the pasture.

Here I stopped the car and snoozed while two small children crawled all over me.

Here I reread *Moby Dick* (skimming big chunks, even though to me it is the greatest of all novels) in a single day, while Fergus fished.

Here I abandoned the car because of a clonk in the motor and hitchhiked (which in those days in Vermont meant walking the whole way with a limp) all the way to a garage where I passed the afternoon with ex-loggers who had stopped by to oil the joints of their artificial limbs.

Here a barn burned down to the snow. "Friction," one of the ex-loggers said. "Friction?" "Yup, the mortgage, rubbing against the insurance policy."

Here I went eighty but was in no danger of arrest, for I was "blessed speeding" — trying to get home in time to see my children before they slept.

Here I bought speckled brown eggs with bits of straw shitted to them.

Here I brought home in the back seat two piglets who rummaged inside the burlap sack like pregnancy itself.

Here I heard on the car radio Handel's concerto for harp and lute for the second time in my life, which Inés played to me the first time, making me want to drive after it and hear it forever.

Here I hurt with mortal thoughts and almost recovered.

Here I sat on a boulder by the winter-steaming river and put my head in my hands and considered time — which is next to nothing, merely what vanishes, and yet can make one's elbows nearly pierce one's thighs.

Here I forgot how to sing in the old way and listened to frogs at dusk make their more angelic croaking.

Here the local fortune teller took my hand and said, "What is still possible is inspired work, faithfulness to a few, and a last love, which, being last, will be like looking up and seeing the parachute dissolving in a shower of gold."

Here is the chimney standing up by itself and falling down, which tells you you approach the end of the road between here and there.

Here I arrive there.

Here I must turn around and go back and on the way back look carefully to left and to right.

For here, the moment all the spaces along the road between here and there — which the young know are infinite and all others know are not — get used up, that's it.

THE ANGEL

This angel, who mediates between us
and the world underneath us, trots ahead
so cheerfully. Now and then she bends
her spine down hard, like a dowser's branch,
over some, to her, well-known splashing spot
of holy water, of which she herself in turn
carefully besoms out a thrifty sprinkle.
Trotting ahead again, she scribbles her spine's
continuation into immaterial et cetera,
thus signaling that it is safe for us now
to go wagging our legs along vertically as we do,
across the ups and downs under which lie
ancestors dog-toothed millennia ago into oblivion.
Tonight she will crouch at the hearth,
where demons' breaths flutter up among the logs,
gnawing a freshly unearthed bone — bone of a dog,
if possible — making logs and bone together
cry through the room, crack! splinter! groan!

MIDDLE OF THE NIGHT

A telephone rings through the wall.
Nobody answers. Exactly how
the mouth shapes itself inside
saying the word "gold" is what sleep
would be like if one were happy.
So Kenny Hardman and George Sykes
called "Gaw-way-ay!" at the back
of the house. If I didn't come out
they would call until nightfall,
like summer insects. Or like
the pay phone at the abandoned
filling station, which sometimes
rang, off and on, an entire day.
The final yawn before one sleeps
is the word "yes" said too many times,
too rapidly, to the darkness. On the landing
she turned and looked back. Something
of the sea turtle heavy with eggs,
looking back at the sea. The shocking dark
of her eyes blew alive in me
the affirmative fire. It would have hurt
to walk away, just as it would bewilder
a mouth making the last yawn to say "no."

CONCEPTION

Having crowed the seed
of the child of their hearts
into her in the dark middle
of the night, as cocks
sometimes cry out to a light
not yet visible to the rest,
and lying there with cock
shrugging its way out of her,
and rising back through phases
of identity, he hears
her say, "Yes, I am two now,
and with thee, three."

THE SOW PIGLET'S ESCAPES

When the little sow piglet squirmed free,
Gus and I ran her all the way down to the swamp
and lunged and floundered and fell full-length
on our bellies stretching for her — and got her! —
and lay there, all three shining with swamp slime —
she yelping, I laughing, Gus — it was then I knew
he would die soon — gasping and gasping.
She made her second escape on the one day
when she was just big enough to dig an escape hole
and still small enough to squeeze through it.
Every day for the next week I took a bucket of meal
to her plot of rooted-up ground in the woods,
until one day there she was, waiting for me,
the wild beast evidently all mealed out of her.
She trotted over and let me stroke her back
and, dribbling corn down her chin, put up her little worried
    face
as if to remind me not to forget to recapture her —
though, really, a pig's special alertness to death
ought to have told her: in Sheffield the dolce vita
leads to the Lyndonville butcher. But when I seized her
she wriggled hard and cried, wee wee wee, all the way home.

THE OLIVE WOOD FIRE

When Fergus woke crying at night
I would carry him from his crib
to the rocking chair and sit holding him
before the fire of thousand-year-old olive wood,
which it took a quarter-hour of matches
and kindling to get burning right. Sometimes
— for reasons I never knew and he has forgotten —
even after his bottle the big tears
would keep on rolling down his big cheeks
— the left cheek always more brilliant than the right —
and we would sit, some nights for hours,
rocking in the almost lightless light
eking itself out of the ancient wood,
and hold each other against the darkness,
his close behind and far away in the future,
mine I imagined all around.
One such time, fallen half-asleep myself,
I thought I heard a scream
— a flier crying out in horror
as he dropped fire on he didn't know what or whom,
or else a child thus set aflame —
and sat up alert. The olive wood fire
had burned low. In my arms lay Fergus,
fast asleep, left cheek glowing, God.

MILK

When he pulls back on the oars
slightly too large for him, the boat
surges forward, toward the island
where he picks up the milk bottle
the old man he's never seen
puts out at the end of the dock;
toward the shore by the highway
where he exchanges four empty
milk bottles for the four full
the milkman he's never seen either
sets down to glow at roadside;
toward the dock where he leaves
one full bottle for the old man;
toward home across lake water
around which the shore trees stand
right side up in the world
and upside down in the world under it,
into which utterly still moments
are the doors childhood almost opens,
bringing back milk in time for breakfast.

LAKE MEMPHREMAGOG

We loaf in our gray boat in the sunshine.
The Canadian Pacific freight following the shoreline blows a
    racket of iron over Lake Memphremagog.
The children cast, the fishes do not bite.
They leap into the water and splash, the Memphremagog monster
    does not bite.
Far off, in the center of Newport, the train again blows, one after
    one, all its five sad horns of diesel.
Long ago I astonished my own cheeks with the amount of tears
    one child can cry.
It's frightening that those nights now lie almost farther away than
    memory goes.
All the elsewheres, so far away, where children cry, where mothers
    and fathers cry for their children, as the train's cries fade,
    fade.
Our boat lies very still in the Memphremagog water, and it's still.
Here everybody is O.K.
I am fifty. The children are just little ones.

THE MAN SPLITTING WOOD
IN THE DAYBREAK

The man splitting wood in the daybreak
looks strong, as though, if one weakened,
one could turn to him and he would help.
Gus Newland was strong. When he split wood
he struck hard, flashing the bright steel
through air of daybreak so fast rock maple
leapt apart — as they think marriages will
in countries about to institute divorce —
and even willow, which, though stacked
to dry a full year, on separating
actually weeps — totem wood, therefore,
to the married-until-death — miseried asunder
with many small lip-smacking gasp-noises.
But Gus is dead. We could turn to our fathers,
but they protect us only through the unperplexed
looking-back of the numerals cut into their headstones.
Or to our mothers, whose love, so devastated,
can't, even in spring, break through the hard earth.
Our spouses weaken at the same rate we do.
We have to hold our children up to lean on them.
Everyone who could help goes or hasn't arrived.
What about the man splitting wood in the daybreak,
who looked strong? That was years ago. That was me.

THE FROG POND

In those first years I came down
often to the frog pond — formerly,
before the earthen dam gave way,
the farm pond — to bathe, standing
on a rock and throwing pond water over me,
and doing it quickly because of the leeches,
who need but minutes to know you're there,
or to read the mail or to scribble
or to loaf and think — sometimes of the future —
while the one deer fly
that torments every venturer into July
in Vermont — smack it dead as often
as one will — buzzed about my head.
A few years after I got here, the beavers came,
pointed rows of sharpened sticks
at the water and made it rise,
and the frog pond became the beaver pond.
The next year an old rowboat appeared,
with sheet metal nailed all around it
to hold the hull boards in place
while they rotted. The four
of us would oar, pole, and bale out
a few feet above the sunken green bank
where a man used to sit and think
and look up and seem to see four people
up here oaring and poling and baling out
above him: the man *seems* happy,
the two children laugh and splash,
a slight shadow crosses the woman's face

as though she must wait for him. Then
one spring the beavers disappeared—
trapped off, or else gone away
on their own to make a pond elsewhere —
in which case this pond and that one
and the next, one after one, will flow off,
each leaving behind its print
in the woods, a sudden green meadow
with gleams of sky meandering through it.
The man who lies propped up
on an elbow, scribbling in a notebook
or loafing and thinking, will be older
and will remember this place held a pond once,
writhing with leeches and overflown
by the straight blue bodies of dragonflies,
and will think of smallest children
grown up and of true love broken
and will sit up abruptly and swat
the hard-biting deer fly on his head,
crushing it into his hair, as he has done before.

THE OLD LIFE

The waves collapsed into themselves
with heavy rumbles in the darkness
and the soprano shingle whistled
gravely its way back into the sea.
When the moon came from behind clouds
its white full-moon's light
lightly oiled the little beach stones
back into silence. We stood
among shatterings, glitterings,
the brilliance. For some reason
to love does not seem ever
to hurt any less. Now it happens
another lifetime is up for us,
another life is upon us.
What's left is what is left
of the whole absolutely love-time.

PART II

PRAYER

Whatever happens. Whatever
what is is is what
I want. Only that. But that.

THE FERRY STOPPING AT MACMAHON'S POINT

It comes vigorously in,
nudges the jetty and ties up,
the usually ill-tossed line tossed twice,
presses by engine pressure against
the pilings for its half-minute passed
in the young's leaps and the old's totters,
backs out, turns, and prow lifted
like the head of a swimming dog,
makes for the Lavender Bay jetty.

MOUNT FUJI AT DAYBREAK

From the Fuji-view stand made of cinder block
a crow watches Fuji rise into daybreak.
Trash smoke light-blues the exhausted valley.
Hot-spring steam blows up out of steam holes.
Up the road out of town a tanker truck groans.
An electric bullhorn now crackles messages
to workers coming early out of their doors.
From the cinder block Fuji-view stand the crow
flies off repeating the round vowel "ah!"
to Mount Fuji now risen bright into daybreak,
or else — who can say? — "ha! ha! ha! ha!"

BREAK OF DAY

He turns the light on, lights
the cigarette, goes out on the porch,
chainsaws a block of green wood down the grain,
puts the pieces into the box stove,
pours in kerosene, tosses in the match
he set fire to the next cigarette with,
stands back while the creosote-lined, sheet-
metal rust-lengths shudder but manage
to lure the *cawhoosh* from inside the stove,
which sucks in ash motes through holes at the bottom
and glares out fire blaze through cracks around the top,
all the way to the roof and up out through
into the still starry sky starting to fade,
sits down to a bowl of crackers and blue milk
in which reflections of a 40-watt ceiling bulb
suicide-attempt, eats, contemplates
an atmosphere containing kerosene stink,
chainsaw smoke, chainsmoke, wood smoke, wood heat,
gleams of a 40-watt ceiling bulb trying to drown.

FARM PICTURE

Black earth
turned up, clods
shining on their
western sides, hay
sprouting on top
of bales of spoiled
hay, an old
farmer bent far
over like *Australopithecus
robustus*, carrying two dented
pails of water out
to the hen yard.

SOME SONG

On a stoop
the old man
is drinking him
some beer,
the boy in
his yellow shirt
is playing
him some banjo tune,
the old fellow
hasn't any
teeth, and the boy
sings him, yes,
some song.

COINALISTE

She can drink from a beer bottle.
She can light a cigar and sneeze out the match.
She can drag on it so hard the end blazes.
She can inhale without coughing.
She can blow a smoke ring or two.
She can withdraw and introspect.

She can play the nose flute: $\bar{f}\sharp$ with lower hole unstopped; $\bar{a}$ with
both holes unstopped; $\bar{c}\sharp$ with both stopped: the tonic, the
mediant, the dominant of the chord of F$\sharp$ major.
She can suck the whole instrument inside, where it continues to
sing and cry.
She can speak a pouting, pidgin blabber.

She can clench on the ictus and moan on the arsis but can't come
on the thesis.
She can wink and throw French kisses.
She can motherly-kiss the fuzzy cheeks of young sailors.
She can pick up the money they toss, including the dollar bills.
She can count but not give change.
She can smile.

DRIFTWOOD FROM A SHIP

It is the white of faces from which the sunburn has suddenly been
scared away.

It has the rounded shoulders of those who fear they will pass the
rest of their days alone.

The final moments of one it couldn't hold up—possibly the cook,
who possibly could neither cook nor swim—have been gasped
into it.

The black residue inside the black holes—three set close together,
three far apart, three close—remembers the hammer blows'
downward stages, which shined nine nails permanently into
their vanishing places.

A plane's long, misericording *shhhhhhhh*'s long ago soothed away
the halo fragments the sawmill's circular saw had tormented
across its planes.

The pebbles it rubs itself into fuzz up all over it a first beard,
white right from the start.

Its grain cherishes the predicament of spruce, which has a trunk
that rises and boughs that fall.

Its destiny is to disappear.

This could be accomplished when a beachcomber extracts its heat
and resolves the rest into smoke and ashes; or in the normal
way, through combined action of irritation and evanescence.

FIRE IN LUNA PARK

The screaming produced by the great fright machines —
one like a dough beater that lifts, turns, plunges the victims
strapped to its arms,
one a huge fluted pan that tries to whirl its passengers off the earth,
one that holds its riders upside down and pummels them until the
screams pour out freely,
while above them the roller coaster, before it plunges, creeps
seemingly lost among its struts and braces
and under them the Ghost Train jerks through tunnels here and
there lighted by fluorescent bones —
has fallen still today.

To us who live on Lavender Bay,
formerly Hulk Bay, before that no one now knows what,
it seemed the same easily frightened, big-lunged screamer vibra-
toed in mock terror each night across the water, and we hardly
heard and took no notice.
But last night the screams pierced through dinner parties' laugh-
ter, lovemaking's crying, Mozart's laughing-and-crying, and kept
at it, until we sat up startled.

The Ghost Train, now carrying seven souls and the baffled grief
of families,
has no special destination,
but must wander looking for forgetfulness through the natural
world,
where all are born, all suffer, and many scream,
and no one is healed but gathered and used again.

THE GEESE

As soon as they come over the mountain
into the Connecticut valley and see the river
they will follow until nightfall,
bodies, or cells, begin to tumble
between the streamers of their formation,
thinning the left, thickening the right,
until like a snowplowing skier the flock shifts weight
and shaking with its inner noises
turns, and yahonks and spirit-cries
toward that flow of light spelled into its windings
endlessly ago — each body flashing white
against the white sky when the wings lift,
and black when they fall, the invisible
continuously perforating the visible —
and trembles away, to vanish, but before that
to semi-vanish, as a mirage
or deepest desire does when it gets
the right distance from us and becomes rhythmic.

THE SHROUD

Lifted by its tuft
of angel hairs, a milkweed
seed dips-and-soars
across a meadow, chalking
in outline the rhythm
that waits in air all along,
like the bottom hem of nowhere.
Spinus tristis, who spends
his days turning gold
back into sod, rises-and-falls
along the same line the seed
just waved through the sunlight.
What sheet or shroud large enough
to hold the whole earth
are these seamstresses' chalks
and golden needles
stitching at so restlessly?
When will it ever be finished?

PART III

CHAMBERLAIN'S PORCH

On three sides of the stretcher bed
where I half sleep, rainwater runs down
boughs all broken out in buds out there
in the world the porch screen cuts up
into tiny, very perishable rectangles.
Rain putters down on the wood shingles overhead,
now smattering heavily, becoming
a language I think I will learn one day,
now slackening, making the sounds
of delicate kissings between one and one,
which some memorize even into the grave;
as though the mechanism governing the inner
pluckings of things, which goes forward forever,
pauses to try out its backward variations
on this wood-shingled porch roof in Connecticut.
Very distinctly, close to my ear,
a child's voice whispers "Grandpa!" A grandchild
still to be found? Or me, long ago,
calling an already lost grandfather?
Rain flurries down suddenly very thick,
overall batterings of the first shovelfuls
on a roof under which only a body half listens.

CEMETERY ANGELS

On these cold days
they stand over
our dead, who will
erupt into flower as soon
as memory and human shape
rot out of them, each bent
forward and with wings
partly opened as though
warming itself at a fire.

DECEMBER DAY IN HONOLULU

This day, twice as long as the same day in Sheffield, Vermont,
     where by five the stars come out,
gives the postman opportunity to boggle the bell thrice.
First, a letter from Providence lamenting the "siege against poets"
     — Wright, Rukeyser, Hayden.
Next, Richard Hugo's memoir of James Wright, which says, "Yes.
     I knew him. I loved him."
Last, around the time of stars in Sheffield, a package holding four
     glass doorknobs packed in a *New York Times* of a year ago,
     which Muriel Rukeyser had sea-mailed to me, to fulfill if not
     explain those mysterious words she used to whisper whenever
     we met: "Galway, I have your doorknobs."
The wail of a cat in heat — in ultraheat, I should say, here every-
     thing is hot already — breaks in, like the voice of propagation
     itself:
This one or that one dies but never the singer: whether in Hono-
     lulu in its humid mornings or in New York in its unbreathable
     dusk or in Sheffield now dark but for chimney sparks dying into
     the crowded heaven, one singer falls but the next steps into the
     empty place and sings . . .
The wail comes more heavily. Maybe propagation itself must haul
     its voice all the way up from the beginning.
Or it could be it's just a very old cat, clanking its last appearance
     on the magic circle of its trash can lid, from its final life crying
     back — before turning totally faithful forever — an earlier, per-
     haps the first, life's first, irreplaceable lover.

35

ON THE OREGON COAST

In memoriam Richard Hugo

Six or seven rows of waves struggle landward.
The wind batters a pewtery sheen on the water between them.
As each wave makes its way in, most of it gets blown back out to
    sea, subverting even necessity.
The bass rumble of sea stones, audible when the waves flee all
    broken back out to sea, itself blows out to sea.
Now a log maybe thirty feet long and six across gets up and
    trundles down the beach.
Like a dog fetching a stick it flops unhesitatingly into the water.
An enormous wave at once sends it wallowing back up the beach
    again.
It lies among other driftwood, almost panting. Sure enough, after
    a few minutes it gets up, trundles down the beach, throws itself
    into the water again.
The last time I was on this coast Richard Hugo and I had dinner
    together just north of here, in a restaurant overlooking the sea.
The conversation came around to personification.
We agreed that eighteenth- and nineteenth-century poets almost
    had to personify, it was like mouth-to-mouth resuscitation, the
    only way they could imagine to keep the world from turning
    into dead matter.
And that as post-Darwinians it was up to us to anthropomorphize
    the world less and animalize, vegetablize, and mineralize our-
    selves more.
We doubted that pre-Darwinian language would let us.
Our talk turned to James Wright, how his kinship with salaman-
    ders, spiders and mosquitoes allowed him to drift back down
    through the evolutionary stages.

When a group of people gets up from a table, the table doesn't
   know which way any of them will go.
James Wright went back to the end. So did Richard Hugo.
The waves coming in burst up through their crests and fly very
   brilliant back out to sea.
The log gets up yet again, goes rolling and bouncing down the
   beach, plunges as though for good into the water.

LAST HOLY FRAGRANCE

In memoriam James Wright

When by first light I went out
from the last house on the chemin de Riou
to start up the cistern pump, there he sat,
mumbling into his notebook at an upstairs window
while the valley awakened: a cock
called full force, a car's gears
mis-shifted, a dog made some feeble yaps.
The next winter in Mt. Sinai, voiceless,
tufted with the shavelessness that draggles
from chins on skid row in St. Paul,
Minnesota, he handed me the poem
of that Vence morning. Many times since,
I have read it and each time I have heard
his voice saying it under my voice,
and in fact in those auditoriums
that don't let you "hear yourself," sometimes
I hear only his voice, edged, pitying,
surprising language with the mourning
that goes on inside it, for what it names,
making my eyes "pop" a little, perhaps
showing the whites, as his used to,
when the poems were at their saddest.
But poetry sings past even the sadness
that begins it: the drone of poetry readings
or the mutterings coming from poets' workrooms —
as oblivious to emotion as the printed page —
are only seeking that chant of the beginning,
older than any poem, that the song men
of Arnhem Land, who jolt their clapsticks

with a rebuking force like a spank, think
they summon, or the shaman in Point Barrow,
Alaska, having trance-learned it, translates,
or gopher frogs put to us in *parallelismus membrorum*,
or, now and then, a pure poem glories in.
As do those last, saddest poems of his,
which overtake the chant, synchronize
with its happiness, and, as when first light blooms
clouds of night, give us *mourning*'s morning.
"How am I ever going to be able to say this?
The truth is there is something terrible,
almost unspeakably terrible in our lives,
and it demands respect, and, for some reason
that seems to me quite insane, it doesn't hate us.
There, you see? Every time I try
to write it down it comes out gibberish."
When the song goes, silence replaces it
inside the bones. He lies back fast asleep
in the airplane seat. Under his eyelids
consciousness flickers. What's happening?
A computation: the difference, figured
in a flash, between what has been lived
and what remains to be. He dreams perhaps
of whittling a root, transfiguring it
by subtraction — of whatever it is in roots
that makes them cling — perhaps into a smile,
which now passes his lips, or else into
a curled up, oriental death's body
mummified into the memories of his last visitors.
Even fast asleep his face is a-sweat. SS
torturers start working Cagney over. He knows
he will soon crack and spill the invasion plans.
When he hears the rumbling of the B-24s
come to shut his mouth, he cracks a grin.
When the bombs start exploding about him,
he throws back his head and madly laughs.
Sitting up, he peers out the plane window

to see if we might be coming in too low,
ready himself to laugh among all the screams.
For this poet, the blessed moment
was not only at the end, in Fano, in spring,
where, with his beloved Annie, just before
returning home to die, he got well,
but also at first, forty years earlier,
by the Ohio, where he sat still and watched
the river flow, and flowed himself inside it,
humming and lulling first beginnings
that would heal not only his dumb-born self
but also the solitaries mute until death
who sprawl cast-down stupid on sidewalks
like dropped flowers waiting to be dirty-shoesoled
into first perfume or last stink, the same smell,
or squat in their own leakage on curbstones,
watching paper trash gyre and whirlwind
spellbound a block or so down East 12th Avenue
and fall back, trash again, or still stand
on a windy corner, gesticulating and talking
to nobody. The computation darkens.
Again and again it showed plenty of time.
Now, even on the abacus of the rosary,
or the petals, hushed to the tabletop, of roses,
which we mortal augurers figure and refigure
it out on our incredulous infinity of times,
it comes out: a negative number. Fear,
the potion of death, is yet a love derivative,
and some terrible pinch of it must be added
to restore the clingingness the penknife
gouges off the root. Near where it first forms,
the Ohio stops in its bed and holy-waters under ice
all its creatures, even, in his anticipation,
the boy sitting soon in nobody's memory
some days downriver. He went away,
three-quarters whittled root of silenus wood,
taking a path that, had it simply vanished,

we could imagine keeps going, toward a place
where he waits — in winding-cloth or swaddling-sheet,
death's body but also fetus of new being — to rise again
into the religion of the idolatry of images
graven their moment into being-born-and-dying.
But the path ends there where a white rose
lies on top of its shadow in Martin's Ferry,
Ohio, let drop on her way to church by a child
too stunned by dead bells pounding through sunlight
to hold it, or anything, or anyone, tight
that day, giving up its last holy fragrance
into this ending-time, when the earth
lets itself be shoveled open to take in a body.
It will be a long time before anyone comes
who can lull the words he will not now ever use
— words which, now he has left, turn this way and that —
hum and coax them to press up against,
shape themselves by, know, true-love, and idolize.

THE PAST

A chair under one arm,
a desktop under the other,
the same Smith-Corona
on my back I even now batter
words into visibility with,
I would walk miles,
assemble my writing stall,
type all day, many sheets
of prose and verse all blown
away, while herring gulls
and once a sightseeing plane
turned overhead. The lean-
to of driftwood that thirty-
three-and-a-third years back
I put up on this spot
leans all the way down,
all its driftwood re-drifts.
Spray jumps and blows.
A few gulls fly that way,
a few this. A single duck
whettles out to sea
in straight flight — only vector
of purpose. As for the Quonset hut
I broke into without breaking it
when the storms came, it too
has gone, swept out, burned up,
buried under, nobody knows. Too
bad. But for me not all
that bad. For of the four

possibilities — from *me-and-it-
still-here* to *it-and-me-
both-gone* — this one, *me-here-
it-gone*, is second best,
and will do, for me, for now.
But I wanted it still to be here.
I wanted to sit at the table
and look up and see the sea spray
and beach grass happy together.
I wanted to remember the details:
the dingy, sprouted potatoes,
the Portuguese bread, the Bokar coffee,
the dyed oranges far from home,
the water tasting of decayed aluminum,
the kerosene stench. The front
steps where I sat and heard
the excitement that comes into sand,
the elation into poverty grass,
when the wind rises. In a letter
which cast itself down in General
Delivery, Provincetown, my friend
and mentor warned, "Don't lose
all touch with humankind." One day
while all around gulls whistled
their thin, exhausted screams,
the wind put down a sudden sheen
or flatness like spiritual quietness
across the water. Now two
waves of the North Atlantic
roll in side by side,
converge, ripple into one
and rush up the beach — making me
jump back — and vanish
under white bubbles all suddenly
popping away at once. Here
waves slap not in time
but in evanescence, a rhythmless medium.

43

Mere comings, mere goings. Though now
there's somewhat less coming
in the comings and considerably more
going in the goings. Between
the two straggles only
such an indicated boundary as the sea
lets the moon spell and die out
between world and world,
a wandering thread solitary walkers
follow along a beach, cross
and recross, spinning it
with their tracks all the way
into disappearance. So you see,
to reach the past is easy. A snap.
A snap of the sea and a third of a century
passes. All nothing. Or all all,
if that sounds more faithful. But anyway
all gone. The work of
whoziwhatzit — Zeit . . . Zman . . . Chas . . .
whatever . . . Whichever
you strike with the desperate tongue
gives a deadened sound, as though
the thing itself were fake; or unspeakable.

FIRST DAY OF THE FUTURE

They always seem to come up
on the future, these cold, earthly dawns;
the whiteness and the blackness
make the flesh shiver as though it's starting to break.
But that is always just an illusion,
always it is just another day they illuminate
of the permanent present. Except for today.
A motorboat sets out across the bay,
a transfiguring spirit, all its little puffy gasps
of disintegration collected
and anthemed out in a pure purr of dominion.
It disappears. In the stillness again
the shore lights remember the dimensions of the black water.
I don't know about this new life.
Even though I burned the ashes of its flag again and again
and set fire to the ticket that might have conscripted me into its
    ranks forever,
even though I squandered all my talents composing my emigra-
    tion papers,
I think I want to go back now and live again in the present time,
    back there
where someone milks a cow and jets of intensest nourishment go
    squawking into a pail,
where someone is hammering, a bit of steel at the end of a stick
    hitting a bit of steel, in the archaic stillness of an afternoon,
or somebody else saws a board, back and forth, like hard labor
in the lungs of one who refuses to come to the very end.
But I guess I'm here. So I must take care. For here

one has to keep facing the right way, or one sees one dies, and
   one dies.
I'm not sure I'm going to like it living here in the future.
I don't think I can keep on doing it indefinitely.

THE FUNDAMENTAL PROJECT
OF TECHNOLOGY

"A flash! A white flash sparkled!"
  Tatsuichiro Akizuki, *Concentric Circles of Death*

Under glass: glass dishes which changed
in color; pieces of transformed beer bottles;
a household iron; bundles of wire become solid
lumps of iron; a pair of pliers; a ring of skull-
bone fused to the inside of a helmet; a pair of eyeglasses
taken off the eyes of an eyewitness, without glass,
which vanished, when a white flash sparkled.

An old man, possibly a soldier back then,
now reduced down to one who soon will die,
sucks at the cigarette dangling from his lip, peers
at the uniform, scorched, of some tiniest schoolboy,
sighs out bluish mists of his own ashes over
a pressed tin lunch box well crushed back then when
the word *future* first learned, in a white flash, to jerk tears.

On the bridge outside, in navy black, a group
of schoolchildren line up, hold it, grin at a flash-pop,
scatter like pigeons across grass, see a stranger, cry
hello! hello! hello! and soon *goodbye! goodbye!*
having pecked up the greetings that fell half unspoken
and the going-sayings that those who went the day
it happened a white flash sparkled did not get to say.

If all a city's faces were to shrink back all at once
from their skulls, would a new sound come into existence,
audible above moans eaves extract from wind that smoothes

the grass on graves, or raspings heart's-blood greases still,
or wails infants trill born already skillful at the grandpa's rattle,
or infra-screams bitter-knowledge's speechlessness
memorized, at that white flash, inside closed-forever mouths?

To de-animalize human mentality, to purge it of obsolete
evolutionary characteristics, in particular of death,
which foreknowledge terrorizes the contents of skulls with,
is the fundamental project of technology; however,
pseudologica fantastica's mechanisms require:
to establish deathlessness it is necessary to eliminate
those who die; a task attempted, when a white flash sparkled.

Unlike the trees of home, which continually evaporate
along the skyline, the trees here have been enticed down
toward world-eternity. No one knows which gods they enshrine.
Does it matter? Awareness of ignorance is as devout
as knowledge of knowledge. Or more so. Even though not knowing,
sometimes we weep, from surplus of gratitude, even though
        knowing,
twice already on earth sparkled a flash, a white flash.

The children go away. By nature they do. And by memory,
in scorched uniforms, holding tiny crushed lunch tins.
All the ecstasy-groans of each night call them back, satori
their ghostliness back into the ashes, in the momentary shrines,
the thankfulness of arms, from which they will go
again and again, until the day flashes and no one lives
to look back and say, a flash, a white flash sparkled.

THE WAKING

What has just happened between the lovers,
who lie now in love-sleep under the memory
of owls calling in the deeper love-sleep of the woods —
call exhaled, *answer* inhaled, *call* exhaled,
answer inhaled, back and forth, and so on,
until one, calling faster, overtakes the other
and the two suddenly whoo together in a single
shimmering harmonic — is called "lovemaking."
But lovers who come exalted to their trysts,
who come to each other from opposite directions
along a path by the sea, through the pines,
meet, embrace, go up from the sea,
make love, lie crushed into each other
under the all-golden sky already deep-blueing
its moon and stars into shining, know
they don't "make" love, which is, was, will be,
but are earth-creatures chosen by moon-pull
to live and flow and — here no other word will do —
fuck one another forever if possible across the stars.
But this word, perhaps first heard when lovers
dropped a stone into the sea at night
and out in the dark a mullet leapt and fell back,
sounding an answer that reverberated in them,
has had the map of the almost-last pathway left
craving its way back to the beginning sinned out of it.
The true word, if it exists, exists *inside* the tongue
and from there must make every word, even consciousness,
even all of forgetting, remember: as when
flamingoes change feeding places on a marsh

and there is a moment — after the first to fly
has put its head underwater in the new place
and before in the old place the last
lifts its head to see the rest have gone —
when, scattered with pink bodies, the sky
becomes all one vast remembering. They still hear,
in the distance, the steady crushing and uncrushing
of bedsprings; and perhaps only imagine a sonata
in which violins' lines remember into the room
the writhing and shifting of sexual bodies.
The already-memory of what has just happened
is their *déjà-prévu* of the existence
of existence. They lie with heads touching,
thinking themselves back across the blackness
that converts back to use of world-light
those who have lived one moment by love-light.
On the brightening sheet their bodies re-form
— golden heaps the true embrace ripple-sluiced
out of the night. The bed, caressed threadbare,
worn almost away, is now one more place on earth
where such inner light as humans can shine with
seeps up into us. The eyelids,
which love the eyes and must lie-on-them to sleep,
open: *This is a bed. That is a fireplace.*
That is last morning's breakfast tray,
which nobody has yet bothered to take away.
This face — too rich in feeling to have lived past
the world in which it is said, "Ni vous sans moi,
ni moi sans vous," so blatantly archaic
this day might be breaking in the Middle Ages —
is the illusion randomness chooses
to smile into existence, now, on this pillow.
The lovers don't have words to know this through.
The scraps of poetry they do have mean less
in the in-the-tongue language than "want a cracker"
or "pieces of eight" in ours. Through tears
they see more truly than the dry-eyed the motes

cross, mingle, collide, lose their way, in this puff
of ecstatic dust. Now the tears overwhelm the eyes,
wet their faces, drain quickly away
into their smiles. One leg hangs off the bed.
He is still inside her. His big toe
sticks into the pot of strawberry jam. "Oh migod!"
They laugh. They have to remind themselves how to.
They kiss while laughing and hit teeth
and remember they are bones and at once laugh
naturally again. A clock is ticking. The feeling —
perhaps it is only a feeling, perhaps due
to living always in the same lifetime
with only dying things — that time passes,
comes over them. They get up,
put on clothes, go out. They are not in the street
yet, however, but for a few moments longer
still in their elsewhere, on a riverbank
standing with their arms around each other in the aura
the earth has when it remembers its former beauty.
Something in them — the past — belongs
to the away-going water and must flow away
into time to come forever. It does not yet surprise them
that they are wood-nymph and river-spirit,
who can speak for mute things and name them.
River birds . . . honk. Sounds arrive fully formed
into their mouths . . . *Bleecker* . . . *Carmine* . . . *Avenue*
of the Americas . . . An ambulance sirens
a shroud-whitened body toward St. Vincent's.
A police car running the red lights parodies
in high pitch the owls of paradise. The lovers enter
the ordinary day the ordinary world
providentially provides. Their pockets ring.
Good. For now askers and beggarmen
come up to them needing change for breakfast.

THAT SILENT EVENING

I will go back to that silent evening
when we lay together and talked in low, silent voices,
while outside slow lumps of sky-talk
fell, hushing as they got near the ground,
with a fire in the room, in which centuries
of tree went up in continuous ghost-giving-up,
without a crackle, into morning light.
Not until what hastens went slower did we sleep.
When we came back we turned and looked back
at our tracks, where they lie still across the land
of our twining, twining out of the woods
where the branches we brushed against let fall
puffs of sparkling snow, quickly, in silence,
like stolen kisses, and where the *scritch scritch scritch*
among the trees, which is the sound that dies
inside the sparks that shoot from the wedge when the sledge
hits it off center telling everything inside
it is fire, jumped to a black branch, all puffed up
and without arms, and so obviously lonesome,
and yet — how could we know this? — *happy!*
in shape of chickadee. Lying still in snow,
not iron-willed, like railroad tracks, willing
not to meet until heaven, but here and there
making stomped, slubby kissing-knots in the snow,
our tracks wobble across the field their long scratch.
Everything that happens here — even in the cold air
the chick when at last grown old *dee dee dees*
away through, borne on the mercy, if any,
of time — is really little more, if even that,

than a scratch, too. Words, in the mouth of our mouths,
and in our tongues touching their words as silently,
are almost ready, already, to bandage the one
whom the *scritch scritch scritch*, meaning *if how when*
we will lose each other, scratches scratches scratches
from this moment to that. Then I will go back
to that silent evening, when the past just managed
to overlap the future, if just by a trace, and the light
that lives inside the eclipse doubles and shines
through the darkness the sparkling that heavens the earth.

THE SEEKONK WOODS

When first I walked here I hobbled
along ties set too close together
for a boy to step naturally on each.
When I grew older, I thought, my stride
would reach every other and thereafter
I would walk in time with the way
toward the meeting place of rails
in that yellow Lobachevskian haze up ahead.
Right about here we put down our pennies, dark
on shined steel, where they trembled, fell still,
and waited for the locomotive rattling berserk
wheel-rods into perfect circles out of Attleboro
to brighten them into wafers, the way a fork
mashes into view the inner light of a carrot
in a stew. In this late March sunshine,
crossing the trees at the angle the bow makes
when the violinist effleurages out of the chanterelle
the C three octaves above middle C,
the old vertical birthwood remembers
its ascent lines, shrunken by half, exactly
back down, each tree's on its fallen last summer.
Back then, dryads lived in these oaks;
these rocks were altars, which often asked
blood offerings — but this one, once, bone, too,
the time Billy Wallace tripped and broke out
his front teeth. Fitted with gold replicas,
he asked, speaking more brightly, "What good
is a golden mouth when there's only grass
to eat?" Though it was true Nebuchadnezzar

spent seven years down on all fours eating
vetch and alfalfa, ruminating the mouth-feel
of "bloom" and "wither," earth's first catechism,
until he was healed, nevertheless we knew
if you held a grass blade between both thumbs
and blew hard you could blurt all its shrieks
out of it — like those beseechings leaves oaks
didn't drop last winter just now scratched out
on a least breeze, let-me-die-let-me-die.
Maybe Billy, lured by bones' memory,
comes back sometimes, too, to the Seekonk Woods,
to stand in the past and just look at it.
Here he might kneel, studying this clump of grass,
a god inspecting a sneeze. Or he might stray
into the now untrafficked whistling-lanes
of the mourning doves, who used to call and call
into the future, and give a start, as though,
this very minute, by awful coincidence,
they reach it. And at last traipse off
down the tracks, with stumbling, arrhythmic gait,
as wanderers must do once it hits them:
the over-the-unknown route, too, ends up
right where time wants. On this spot
I skinned the muskrat. I buried the rat.
The musk breezed away. Of the fur
I made a hat, which as soon as put on
began to rot off, and even now stinks
so sharply my scalp crawls. In circles,
of course, keeping to the skull. Though
one day this scrap of damp skin
will crawl all the way off, and the whole organism
follow. But which way? To effuse with musk?
Or rot with rat? Oh no, we don't choose,
there's a law: *As one supremes,*
so one croaks — forever muskrat! When,
a quarter-turn after the sun, the half-moon,
too, goes down and we find ourselves

in the night's night, then somewhere
thereabouts in the dark must be death.
Knowledge beforehand of the end is surely among
existence's most spectacular feats — and yet right here,
on this ordinary afternoon, in these humblest woods,
with a name meaning "black goose" in Wampanoag,
or in modern Seekonkese, "slob blowing fat nose,"
this unlikely event happens — a creature
straggling along the tracks foreknows it.
Then too long to touch every tie, my stride
is now just too short to reach every other,
and so I am to be still the wanderer,
in velocity if not in direction, the hobble
of too much replaced by the common limp
of too little. But I almost got there.
I almost stepped according to the liturgical,
sleeping gods' snores you can hear singing up
from former times inside the ties. I almost
set foot in that border zone where what follows
blows back, shimmering everything, making
walking like sleepwalking, railroad tracks
a lane among poplars on a spring morning,
where a man, limping but blissful, dazedly
makes his way homeward, his lips, which kissing
taught to bunch up like that, blowing
from a night so overfilled with affection
it still hasn't completely finished passing
these few bent strands of hollowed-out air,
haunted by future, into a tune on the tracks.
I think I'm about to be shocked awake.
As I was in childhood, when I battered myself
back to my senses against a closed door,
or woke up hanging out of an upstairs window.
Somnambulism was my attempt to slip
under cover of nightmare across no father's land
and put my arms around a phantasm. If only
I had found a way to enter his hard time

served at labor by day, by night in solitary,
and put my arms around him in reality,
I might not now be remaking him
in memory still; anti-alchemizing bass kettle's
golden reverberations again and again back down
to hair, flesh, blood, bone, the base metals.
I want to crawl face down in the fields
and graze on the wild strawberries, my clothes
stained pink, even for seven years
if I must, if they exist. I want to lie out
on my back under the thousand stars and think
my way up among them, through them,
and a little distance past them, and attain
a moment of nearly absolute ignorance,
if I can, if human mentality lets us.
I have always intended to live forever,
but even more, to live now. The moment
I have done one or the other, I here swear,
I will come back from the living and enter
death everlasting: consciousness defeated.
But I will not offer, no, I'll never
burn my words. Wishful phrases! The once-
poplars creosoted asleep under the tracks
have stopped snoring. What does that mean?
The bow saws at G. A leaf rattles on its tree.
The rails may never meet, O fellow Euclideans,
for you, for me. So what if we groan?
That's our noise. Laughter is our stuttering
in a language we can't speak yet. Behind,
the world made of wishes goes dark. Ahead,
if not tomorrow then never, shines only what is.

Galway Kinnell lives in Vermont and New York City. He has been the director of an adult education program in Chicago, a journalist in Iran, and a field worker for the Congress of Racial Equality in Louisiana. During the past fifteen years he has taught poetry at colleges and universities in this country and in France and Australia. His *Selected Poems*, published in 1982, won the Pulitzer Prize and, with Charles Wright's *Country Music*, the American Book Award. Galway Kinnell is Samuel F. B. Morse Professor of Arts and Science at New York University, where he teaches creative writing.